I0414636

The Wishing Tree

By

Marjorie Darcene Person

This book is a work of fiction. Places, events, and situations in this story are purely fictional. Any resemblance to actual persons, living or dead, is coincidental.

© 2003 by Marjorie Darcene Person.
All rights reserved.

No part of this book may be reproduced, stored in a retrieval system, or transmitted by any means, electronic, mechanical, photocopying, recording, or otherwise, without written permission from the author.

ISBN: 0-7596-8803-6 (e-book)
ISBN: 0- 7596-8805-2 (Paperback)
ISBN: 0-7596-8804-4 (Rocket Book)

This book is printed on acid free paper.

1stBooks - rev. 03/26/03

THE WISH — CHAPTER ONE

Jim and his dog trots down the road. Jim was kind of skinny; his face was long with thick eyebrows. He was a quiet child with soft brown eyes. Jim's dog Sam was brown with white spots. He thought of the essay that his teacher Mrs. Webb wants the class to write a ten pages essay about the year of 1900, 1910, 1920 and on up, and how it were different from the 90s. Why would she wanted the class to write an essay like that for? He wasn't born back then, his grandma was. Besides, she was always telling he and his two older brothers about the old days.

A smile touches Jim's eyes, he will get his grandma to tell him what it was like back then. Jim's face droop and a sad look appear into his eyes. All grandma would say is how she and her sisters and brothers walked five miles to school barefooted, how they had to worked hard around the house, and how they got lots of whipping. Mrs. Webb wants them to write what event took place in one of those years, Mrs. Webb would want to know the facts and the year it happening in, not about grandma's life, he thought.

Why did she wants them to write about one of those years for? What could had happening that could have been so special? Of was each one of the year was education? 1933 came into his mind. He remembered his Aunt Sally telling him something about that year. Franklin Roosevelt was the president, and he held office during the great depression. What kind of depression did they had back then? He couldn't ask his Aunt Sally, she was decease. He couldn't write his essay about that year because he didn't know all the details, and he sure wasn't going to do no research, all that stuffs were too hard.

Mrs. Webb's class supposed to turns in the essays next Thursday, that was the day he wasn't going to school. He's gonna tell his grandma he's sick. "Yeah, that's what I'm going to do," Jim smiled. As they walks by Joe's grocery store he took ten pennies from his pocket and knew that wouldn't buy him a candy bar.

He remembered his grandma telling him and his two brothers last night about her early days, and how candy bars were from a penny to five cents. When she didn't have any money to buy candies, she would go to the wishing tree, and there at its stump would be five, ten, fifteen pennies. She told them she had to tell the tree her wish, skipped around it three times before the tree granted it. Of course he and his two brothers didn't believes that story. But his grandma was so convincing, it was hard not to. But he couldn't tell his brothers he believed it just a little bit, he pretended to be just like they were, too big to be listen to stories like that, they only did it to make their grandmother happy.

Jim wished he could go there, back in his grandma's times just so he could buy a candy bar. But that was useless thinking even for a nine-year-old. These pennies are useless, he thought as he threw them on the ground and he followed Sam across the street to a large tree.

He looked at it, its branches stretch way up in the blue sky. "Boy, she's big," Jim says as if though this was the first time he sets eye on the tree. "Was it truth what his grandma said? Or was it just a story? He kept staring at it his mindful of wonderment; if only it was truth then he could go back in his grandma's times and buy a candy bar, and see what it was like back then, he could really write that essay then.

He stares down the street at his house to see were his two brothers in the front yard. He didn't want them to sees what he was about to do. They'd teases him for believing in a silly story like that. Jim's eyes brighten with excitement as he touched the large tree. Jim closed his eyes and skipped around the tree three times, chanting. "Take me back to grandma's times." "It didn't worked," he said with his eyes still closed, afraid to take a peek. He felt stupid for doing such a thing, his brothers were right he was a sissy. Gosh, how he hated himself for being so silly.

He opened them slowly. "I knew it wouldn't worked!" come on Sam, let's go home before Grandma gets a whip to me!" Sam began to act strange as if though he was seeing an invisible horrify ghost that only he himself could see. He began to whine as if though he was lost and couldn't sniff his way back home.

"What's wrong, boy?" Jim's eyes caught sight of the countryside that Sam was seeing. He couldn't believe his eyes he was so stunned. Jim shuts his eyes for a moment and then opened them as if the strange view would disappear. "Where were they?" he thought. It's a dream, it's got to be."

Jim looked far, The sign said Goodish Street. What city were they in? And how did he and his dog got there? He lived on Goodish Street in Beargrass. But the street wasn't like this one. The street he lived on was pavement, not dirt. The street he lived on had brick houses on both sides of the street. It had a store on the left side of the road, like this with a large tree beside it, but this store was very old. Jim had never seen a store like this one before. on one side of the dirt road was a cotton field with people in it working. He started to go to the field, but he went down the road after Sam. Sam recognized something, he could tell by the way he was rushing toward it. He recognized it, too, and began to walk fast like his dog toward it.

Sam came upon an old yellow house. It was in the same location as Jim's grandma old yellow house was. Jim's mouth hung opened.

"Wow," Jim said. "If I didn't know any better," "I'd say we were home, boy." Bewildered hold his dog's eyes. "I'm confused too, boy."

An old white lady came to the door at the sound of Jim's knock. She was an old lady with deep wrinkles in her forehead. Jim guess she was eighty five the same age as his grandma. Her lips were very thin with deep frown lines around her mouth. She looked at the boy and his dog with a shocking expression.

"Who are you? And where is my grandma, is she here?" "The question is, who are you?" "Jim Perry, and my grandma name is Alice May Moore." "And you're looking for her?" Jim nodded.

"What make you think she's here?" "Ma'am, that is all he could said, and then he lowered his head. How could he answered that question when he didn't know what was going on. The surroundings look so familiar, but it all was so strange. "The only negro person I know by that name is a small child, and she's working over there in that field." Jim stares in the direction she was pointing. "Don't you know, a negro boy doesn't supposed to be seen at the front door of a white person's house?" "Didn't your mother taught you that, boy?"

Jim gave her a hard look. "No, ma'am, she taught me to respect a person, no matter what colored they are." Are you getting smart with me, boy?" "No, ma'am, I'm just telling you what I have been taught." "I'm going to teach you this, and you listen good." You are a negro, you're not white, and you're supposed to show special respect for a white person, you got that, boy!" "My name is Jim, ma'am, and I don't like the way you are beginning to make me feel, and I'll show respect for everyone, not for white only." Don't you know I can have you beaten to death for sassy me, boy?

Jim started to said, no you can't, but a little voice told him to be silent, he wasn't no longer in his world. Jim nodded his head and ran down the road. He was frightened now, being in a strange world that he didn't understand. He and his dog ran into the field where the workers were picking cottons. The workers were dressed in funny looking clothes as if though it was back in the 30s. A lady handed him a sack. "Do you know how to pick cottons, son?" Jim shook his head. "All you had to do is pick the cottons from those plants and put them in this sack, that's all to it," the lady said,

giving the sack to Jim. But he wouldn't take it.

He stares at the lady with recognition as if

though he was seeing a familiar face in her, he

was, his great grandmother. The lady

resembled his grandmother.

A girl had thick eyebrows with pretty

brown eyes. her face was covered with tiny

moles, a large one rest at the right corner of her

upper lip. He smiled, he recognized that face

anywhere he was staring at the face of his

grandmother when she was a child. She

kneeled down and touch Jim's shoe. "Those

tennis shoes are pretty, I ain't never seen tennis

shoes'like those before." Look Dad, her name

is written on her shoes, Reebok."

"I ain't never heard of a girl's name like

that, Reebok," a boy said that stood near by.

He frowned, "and look at those strange clothes

she's wearing." "I'm not a girl!" Jim snapped.

"If you are not a girl, what are those plaits

doing in your hair?" the boy's father asked as

he let out a giggling. The rest of them joined

him. "Tell your mother to comb that nappy

head of yours," the man said still laughing.

"These are not plaits, these are dreadlocks,"

Jim exclaimed.

He walked toward Jim, he paused, and he stood behind his son. He was a tall man, he was tallest ones out there. "Is this Goodish Street?" Jim asked. "Yeah," the man said. Jim frowned and scratch his head. "What town is this?" "Beargrass," the lady said that handed Jim the sack. "Son, are you lost?" The boy's father asked. Jim frowns once again. "I don't know." He looked around him with the frown still on his face. Everything looks strange all except his dog. Jim's eyes rested on the tree afar off. It was just a little way down the road, just a few inches from the store.

In Jim's world the store would be called Joe's grocery store. But now the store was old-timer. He smiles. "It worked, Grandma wasn't lying, the wishing tree really does worked. He looked around him with a smile on his face, taking in each view with a fascinating expression. He smiles once again. "I can't wait till I tell Don and Paul, he thought, and then the smile fade from his lips. They won't believe him. His brothers would just laughs at him and says, "big as you are, believing in baby's stories like that! And they'll tell everyone on the block. He'd have to show them proof, and that is what he's going to do.

He came out of his thought and hear the tall man calling him over. Jim stood in the cotton field alone while the others sits near the tree eating. The kids skipped around the large tree, holding hands while the old man blow his harmonica. He'd blow for a while, and then he'd sing. "Skip around the wishing tree, skip three times, make your wish." Jim reached in his pocket, he could buy two large pieces of candy bars now for five cent each. He'll show the candies to them, and then they'll believe him. But the ten pennies were no longer in his pocket. He threw them away, Jim thought sadly. He had to go to the wishing tree and wish himself back into his times to get the pennies.

The old man stopped singing. The kids stop skipping, but they still were holding hands around the wishing tree. "Are y'all eyes still closed?" the old man asked. "Yeah!" the children yelled.

The old man reached in his pocket and then he began to put coins at the tree's large stump. The kids grasped at the pennies and ran toward the store. Jim reached for some pennies but they were all gone. He followed the kids inside of the store. The products on the shelves were old looking. It fascinate Jim so much, that each goods he picked up he just stare at the way it look and at its price. He couldn't believe that this five pounds of flour cost five cents. The store didn't sell no kinds of meat, Jim wondered where did the people bought their meats from if the stores didn't sell any. After the employees finish their lunch they return to the cotton field.

IT'S NOT A TALE — CHAPTER TWO

A large white man was coming in the field with a long twig. Each child gather around their parents, thinking the twig the man has was for ones of them. "Tom, is that your boy?" "What have you been teaching him, to sass my Mommy?" Answer me!" he barked. The huge man jumped. "Teaches him things that you aren't got no business teaching him!" He's a negro, he's not white, and that's something I can't help. And he will be treated like one"'

He handed the twig to the man. "You take this and put it on that boy for sassing my

Mommy, if you don't I'm going to beat you with it, and that will teach the rest of y'all a lesson."

"You're going to take that from that white man?" "What's wrong with you, when he's a man just like you are?" Jim exclaimed. When Jim saw the expression on Tom's son face he wished he's kept his big mouth shut. Shame held the boy's face, then Jim's gaze met Tom's, Jim had to look away. The man was more ashamed of himself than his son were of him.

"Mr. smith, you know all of my kids, and they are out in this field with me." And you know me, more than anyone, I wouldn't dare teach my kids to talk like that, I'll put a killing on them. "This girl here, I ain't never set eye on her until today." "I'm not a girl," Jim interrupted. "Whose does this boy belongs to?" Mr. Smith asked. "We don't knows," Tom spoken for everyone. "A few minutes ago, he came running into this cotton field, he and his dog." He was asking a lot of questions. "Sir, I think he's lost."

Mr. Smith rested his gaze on Jim. "Is that right?" Jim nodded. "Where are you from?" "You wouldn't know, so why should I tell you?" "Don't you get smart with me!" "Tom, get that boy out of my field, and if I catch you anywhere near here, I'm going to beat you until you can't stand it, now get!"

Jim ran as fast as he could. Jim opened his eyes. His brother stood beside him, shaking him awake. He sat along side the road against the large oak tree. "Grandma sent me to find you, and I found you asleep to this tree, you and this, lazy old dog." "It took me a long time to wake you, you kept saying I've got to get to the tree before he catches me!" What kind of dream was you having?" "It couldn't have been a dream, Jim thought, it was so real.

As Jim followed his brother in the house. He stood in the narrow hall and knock on the door. "Grandma, I found Jim!" He left the door and ran up the staircase. "Come in, Jim." He opens the door and enter the living room, which was kind of small. The large black sofa and the armchair, the same colored blends in with the white walls. The wall held a pictures of Jim's and his two brothers, and there was also a picture of his parents in each other arms. A large lady sits in an armchair talking on the phone. "Yes, it's in the newspapers, Joe is going to cut that large tree down by his store Saturday, he's going to expansion it."

"Grandma?" Jim said. "Stop interrupted me boy, while I'm talking on the phone, you go sit back over there until I finish!" But Jim wouldn't move. "Grandma, Joe can't cut that tree down, it's the wishing tree, he can't cut it down!" Grandma, the wishing tree works, it really does!"

Mrs. Barnes put her hand over the mouth piece of the phone. "No, it don't, child, it's some old tale I made up." "Grandma, it's not a tale, please believe me, it works, it really does!" "Jim you are too big to be acting like that, and to believe in tales like that." I'm sorry

I told you if I'd known it would have affect you like that.

"It's not a tale, Grandma, and you know it."

He held her eyes, he could see it in the reflection of her eyes that she still remember the wishing tree. The old man playing the harmonica, she and the other kids skipping around the wishing tree. The old man called her raisin face, because so many small moles covered her face. Alice May still wore her hair the same way she did when she was a child, in two long pigtails, but now it was mixed with gray.

How did you know?" It was in her face, but she didn't never said those words, she just stare at him in bewilderment. She shook that thought from her face. "Yes, it is, go in the kitchen and check my corn bread, if it's done take it out of the oven." Why is she pretending it's a tale when she know it's not? he thought as he left the room.

His oldest brother Paul was taking the small pan of corn bread from the oven. "I heard you telling Grandma the wishing tree works, Grandma is right, you are too big to believe in stuff like that, there no such thing as a wishing tree." "Yes, it is, and it does so worked!" Jim was afraid to said it out loud. He watched his brother put the pan of corn bread on the table. Why wasn't he tall like Paul, he was sixteen and could pass for twenty. His hair was cut very close.

Jim, himself was short, most people took him to be six year old. He didn't like that at all when they thoughts he was that young. He continued watching his brother; even though the shirt he has on was long sleeved, the muscular in his arms could be seen through the material. He glances at his, they were very small. Paul cut a slice of corn bread with a butter knife and put the butter in the middle, he took a bite. "Who are you looking at, shrimp?" If you want a piece, go get some, but just don't let Grandma know." When Paul left the kitchen Jim wiped a tear from his eye. He hated it when his brothers call him that.

Only ten customers could enter Joe's grocery store, because it was crowded with goods, on the shelves and racks. Joe was five foot eight, he was more on the skinny side. He wore his hair in cornrows with gray at the hairline. His right eye was squint, and one could tell by looking at it he couldn't see a lit out of it. He has a friendly expression and always smiling. He stood behind the counter talking to Jim.

"Joe, you can't cut the wishing tree down."

"And why not? He didn't smile this time, but look more serious than ever. "I get tired of people like you coming in here telling me how to run my business!" Y'all got to realize, I need more space."

"Joe, look at it this way, if you, if you'd cut down the wishing tree." "Oak tree," he interrupted, that's an oak tree, not no wishing tree!" You've got everybody calling that tree that." "Like I was saying, if you'd cut the wishing tree down, you will lose your business." He laughed. "I'm busy, boy, go on home. "Joe, I'm serious, if you'd cut down the wishing tree you'll lose your business, you will."

"Now, listen!" "I said go on home, I don't have time to listening to no little kid who don't know what he's talking about." I've got to help Angelo wait on these customers!"

"Joe, hear the boy out," an elderly man said. "I agree with him. "Go on kid," he said. Jim thanks him with his eyes. "You see, the wishing tree is what got you all these customers." Everyone in the store laugh except the elderly man that stood beside Jim. Jim walks out with his head down.

"Joe, I know what the kid was trying to said," the elderly man begin. "Everyone, young and old, far and near loves to sits under the shade of the wishing tree's, that's how your business has grown. Some comes to touch it, just to gets luck, and some comes to sits under its shade. Look at those guys, playing dice under it, look at those kids playing. Look at those ladies and kids over there, sitting on the ground eating just like they were at a park."

The man stops pointing and took his gaze from the window. "That's why you can't keep nothing in your store; they buy it all." He pointed to himself. "And this is one nigger that loves to come here for that reason, I love to sit under all that shade, and when I need luck, the wishing tree gives it to me."

That night as he lay in bed Jim's thought drift back to his grandma's times, his mind were on Tom, seeing the pain of shamed on his dark face, and his kids seeing what a coward he was. What hurt Tom the most is when he saw it on his oldest son face. How could he get Tom to stand up to Mr. Smith when he was so afraid of him? How? Jim got up, sat on the side of the bed and stepped into his slippers. The moonlight reflect in the window gave his room a bright glow.

He stepped outside of his bedroom and went downstairs. He knocks on his grandma's door. He knew she wasn't asleep because there was a light under her bedroom door. "Come in, Jim." As he enters she was sitting up in bed reading. "Grandma, how did you know it was me?" "Because I can tell your knocks from your brothers's." Boy, what are you doing up this time of hour? And it better be because you're working on your essay! "Are you?" He shook his head, afraid to tell her he haven't started on it. "Grandma, back in your times, if a black person was scared to speak up for himself to a white person, how does he gets the courage to do it?"

Mrs. Barnes stopped reading the bible for a moment and look under eyed at him. "He wouldn't speak up even if he did had the courage." Jim sat on the bed. "But why?" "That's the way things were back then, you just couldn't get a black person to stand up to a white person." Back then, especially in the twenties, didn't no one cares what happened to a black person, that's why some blacks were afraid to speak up for themselves to a white person, even if they knows that person was wrong. If you know you are right, no matter what the situation is, it pays you to confront that person and that person will respect you for doing it." "He will?" Jim exclaimed.

Alice May puts a look on her face as if though she was thinking. "That question you asked me, does it have anything to do with your essay?" "No, ma'am." "You know the student that write the best essay is going to be put in the newspapers." "Annie thinks her grandson is going to win, but we are going to show her, aren't we, boy?"

"Grandma, the wishing tree it works!" "You stop that nonsense about that wishing tree, and put your mind on that essay." Don't you let Annie's grandson win, if you do I won't hear the last of it. She thinks he's so smart, that's all she talked about, and I'm getting sick of it. Always rubbing it in. I wish just once I can brag about one of my grandsons, and when I think I can, she knocks me down. Just like when Paul made a good report card, I went over to her house to showed it to her. She smiled and said. "Oscar made an honorroll, he didn't get nil C, but all A. I see a C on Paul's."

She stared down for a second and then continue. "I was so disappointed, not of Paul, I'm proud of him, but of her." She shouldn't have did that. "I was so pleased that day to show her Paul's report card, and she took the joy from me." I want the best for my grandsons like she wants the best for hers, even though she's got one. But to her, no one can outdo her grandson, she thinks he's better than anyone."

She paused and Jim had to turn his head, he couldn't stand to see his grandmother like that with so much pains on her face. "She made me felt so bad that day." She always brag about him, he round there stealing her money, and she's blaming it on poor Max." She bragged about him too much, I can't get a word in. "Please, baby, makes grandma proud by winning that essay." And then she smiles. I sure would like to see Annie's face when you win that essay." "Grandma, the wishing tree works, it does, why won't you believe me?"

The old lady gave him a strange look. "Jim, I've told you and your brothers that story because I thought y'all would enjoy it like my Betty did when she was a child." Her voice lowered, and Jim could hear the sadness in it. He and his brothers missed their mother too. His mother was under the influence of drug when his parents gotten killed in that car wreck. "Jim, that wishing tree is a made." He cuts her off. "No, it's not, Grandma, it's not a tale!" That old man would played the harmonica, and you and your brothers and sisters and some more kids would skipped around the wishing tree, and y'all eyes will be closed, and when y'all opened them, a whole bunch of pennies will be at the stump of the tree."

Jim smiles and begin to bounce on the bed. "Sang that song about the wishing tree!" "How did you know about Old Limp and his harmonica?" Did you read my diary?" "No, ma'am, I wish myself back into your times, and it took me and Sam there."

She touched the boy's left cheek. "Baby, you was dreaming, and for you to know that kind of information about Old Limp; you read my diary, you have to. "Don't you know if that wishing tree was real, I'd have wish us enough money to pay all these bills, time as my little bit of money comes each month, it's gone, get you a new bike, Don those drum set, and Paul a car. We needs that for the family." She paused for a moment and look around the room. "And yes, I'd wish us a new house, I saw one on Cherry Lane I want. Gosh, I wish that wishing tree did works, that's one house

I'll buy, it's so pretty." But it doesn't works, and that's a fact."

She met Jim's gaze and have to stare down because disappointment held it. "Sometimes a dream can seems so real, especially to a small child, do you understand?" He nodded and left the room. Was his grandma right? He's got to find out whether it was a dream or not. Jim stood in the hall outside of his grandma's bedroom door. The moonlight was bright he could see it reflect its light in the door window, lighted up the hall with its ray. He opened the front door and ran down the street.

THE CHASE — CHAPTER THREE

In the moonlight the large oak tree looks big and spooky. Jim touched it. "You do worked, don't you girl?" "Tom, and Mr. Smith with that long switch, that couldn't have been a dream. "If I catch you anywhere near here, I'm going to beat you until you can't stand it. He swallowed and wipe the sweat from his forehead, he knew Mr. Smith meant it, but that was the chance he's got to take; he's got to see if the wishing tree was real. And most of all he got to see to it that Tom gets back his self respect for himself.

Jim skipped around the large tree three times, "chanting, take me back to my grandma's times." "I guess Grandma was right, it all was a dream." He left the tree and ran down the street, but now the moonlight didn't give him lights only darkness. He turned the knob but the door wouldn't open. He's locked himself out, how stupid can he be! He picked up a small rock and threw it at the top window in the center of the rooftop. "Paul, open the door, if Grandma catches me out here, she's going to get me!" But didn't no one came to the window.

He picked up another one and throw that too. "C'mon, one of y'all, let me in. C'mon guys." He didn't have no choice but to wake up his grandma. Jim went to the side of the house; at the window he knocked on the shutter. "Grandma, it's me, "I came out here to feed Sam, and I got locked outside. Can you let me in?" Jim put his arms behind his back and with his palms he touched his buttock. He just knew he was going to get it. "Who is it?" That wasn't his grandma's voice. Probably it was one of his brothers playing a trick on him. The door opened with a white lady, holding an oil lamp. Jim's eyes widened, and the lady dropped the lamp. It was the same lady he had talk to earlier. "Who is it, Mama?" A male's voice said from inside of the house. "Get him, Will, get that negro boy!" "Oh, my gosh, the porch is burning!" Did that nigger did that?"

Jim ran round the house it was like he knew where he was going. He ran down the dark path. He knows all along the wishing tree works, this wasn't no dream this was real. As he ran along the path he began to hear dogs barking in the distance. He got to the end of the path and pause, he didn't know which way to go. Think," Jim told himself. If he was home at this same spot, which locations would he be facing? It was kind of hard to think when he was scare, darkness surrounding him, and angry men with vicious dogs in the distantly. If he would go left there is another path that would lead him to Rick's house, and if he keeps going, and open glade. He ran in the darkness the spots were totally different now, he didn't know where he was going. "I want to go home, I want to go home to my grandma." He wiped his wet cheeks with his forefinger. He paused for a moment and dry his eyes. If only he could get to the wishing tree he could go home. The dogs were getting closer, he picked up his feet and ran as fast as he could.

He got off the path and begin to breathe hard. When he heard the dogs he ran. Jim didn't know which way he was going, he lost his balance and fell into something wet. He stays under, letting them past, not letting go of his breath not for a moment. He pull himself from the water and just lay at the bank of the lake. Where were he? He didn't know, he got to get up, he's got to keep going with that thought he got to his feet. Afar off he saw a small light. He kept following it until he came to a small old house. his eyelids felt heavy; his legs felt as if though it couldn't hardly carried him.

Jim knocked on the door it opened by a tall black man. Jim looked in the small room. The light he saw in the window was from an oil lamp, sitting on the table. "Boy, what is you doing here?" Tom exclaimed. When he heard dogs barking he says, "are those dogs after you, boy?" "oh, my God!" You can't be seen here, do me and my family will be in big trouble with Mr. Smith, please go, boy, please for my family's sake!"

"He doesn't know I'm here, please let me come in for a moment just to rest." "All right, but you can't stay long." The room was so old Jim smiles as he looked around it, not letting his gaze miss an inch. All the room has were three beds, a stove, a table with an oil lamp. No rug on the worn out floor. One of the bed held a lady, and the other two, the girls were in one of the bed, and the boys were in the other. Jim realized that the old house has one room.

"Reebox, what happened to you? You're all wet. "Let me see if one of my boys got anything you can wear." Wait!" Mr. Tom, you have got to stand up to Mr. Smith, if you do he will respect you for doing it, believe me he will." Please, Mr. Tom, you have got to do it for yourself and your family."

A strange look came upon the man's face. A look that said, a little boy like you telling a grown man like me how to stand up to another man; that was tearing him up inside. Jim could see it on his face. "Let's steps outside, I don't want them to wake up and hear this."

Jim followed the man outside. The man couldn't look Jim in the eye. Jim knows he was too ashamed. Tom talked with his head down as if though he was staring at his feet. Tom raised his head and stare at Jim for a second. "Why is it so important to you that I do this, when I'm just a stranger to you?" Did someone put you up to this to make fun of me?" "No, sir."

"You expect me to believe that?" "I'm no fool." You tell whoever put you up to this, I don't need no snot-nosed child to tell me how to handling my personal business, I handles it the best way I know how!" Was it Hal?" Hell, he's more scary than I am of Mr. Smith." You tell Hal I'm not scare of his black ass, and any other of them loudmouth son of bitches!" I'll beat the hell out of all of them!"

"Sir, it wasn't no one, I'm doing it on my own." "Then why? I need to know that much!" "Let me ask you one, sir." "Why are you afraid to stand up to Mr. Smith when he is a man just like you are?" "None of your damn business!" Tom shouted.

Jim jumped with his hands at his sides trembling slightly. "I need to know, sir." He shuts his eyes as if though he was expecting the huge man to hit him. "He's white and I'm colored that's the difference." Jim opened his eyes. "You're wrong, Mr. Tom, him being white isn't got nothing to do with it, not nothing, and you can't make me believe that!" If he's wrong and you know it, then you go to him and tell him, not let it eat away at you because you're afraid of him. "You're not breaking the law if you speak your mind to another man, whether he's black or white."

He followed Tom's gaze. Tom's oldest son was at the window. The respect for his father was gone, Jim could see that. The boy gave Tom a cold look and then left the window. "He don't look me in the eye no more, his voice begin to tremble. "He don't mind me now." He put his hand over his eyes. "Something fell in my eyes, boy, I want you to know that." Just before he wiped it away Jim saw a tear on the man's left cheek.

A large tall black man came from around the house, pick up Jim and put him over his shoulder. "Let the boy go, Hal, I mean now!"

"No, "Mr. Smith told me if I saw this boy around here, to get him and put him in that pen behind the store, and that's what I'm going to do!"

"Hal, you know what he'll do to that boy!"

"So, he needs his smartass tore up, going around here thinking he knows more than anybody, and look like a damn sissy with all those damn plaits in his head." And the way it looks, it look like he hasn't have a comb in it in mouths, nappy head, bitch!"

He walked off with the boy, wriggling over his shoulder. Tom stood in his front yard with his head down. "Help me!" "Please help me, Mr. Tom!"

Was Mr. Tom coming to his rescue? Jim went to the entrance and peer through the crack of the door, only darkness stares back at him. He turns his head sharply to the sound and shook. He must have fallen to sleep because when he awaken it was morning. He's got to get back into his world before they cut the wishing tree down, and they were going to do it Saturday. He's got to get out of this place today, he's got to. The door opened and shaft of daylight filled the entrance. Hand of a white man's set a plate on the floor. The door closed and darkness once again surrounded him. Please, Mr. Tom, you've got to rescue me. He peered through the crack, it was if though he was peering through a peephole. Jim saw an old building a yard from him. He carried his eye a little farther. Men were sitting in chairs around a large tree. Some were drinking sodas. At one of its long branches, hang a rope.

A smile came on Jim's lips. It was the wishing tree. He reached down and pick up the plate, and began to eat the bacon and eggs, grits. He set the empty plate down, and put his feet against the door. He pushed at it with all of his strength. Why was Mr. Smith keeping him in this pen? It was so small he couldn't stand up in it. He pushed at the door but the old wooden door wouldn't give into his strength.

He took another peer and saw Tom to the pump behind the store, pumping water. He puts his mouth to the pump's mouth and took a mouthful of water. "Mr. Tom!" Mr. Tom!" But the large man ignore the cried of the boy; there was nothing he could do. he took the water pail and walk toward the large oak tree where the six white men sits. He sets the pail on the ground in front of them; his eyes going to the rope, hoping it wasn't for that boy.

"Oh, God, what was he going to do? He's got to get out before Saturday if he didn't he would be stuck into this hateful time. It scare Jim just for being black because it was so deeply hated. For the first time in his life he felt this raw deep fear.

Yes, things were cheap in his grandma's days. A worker had to worked in the field all that week for five dollars. Most of the people burned kerosene lamps because they didn't have electricity. For entertainment they had to listened to radios that ran by batteries. to get back and forth to the store they had to travel on buggies. Those that have vehicles drove old-time cars. And a black person didn't had the freedom that a black person had today. Yes, there still was racism in Jim's world. But there was freedom and a person's rights to do whatever they pleases. That was something no one could take away.

"I want to go home," Jim said, taking his fists and began to rub them into his eyes. He always did that when he was about to cry. Even when he was alone he wouldn't let himself. His oldest brother Paul told him when his grandmother was beating Jim. "Take it like a man, only sissy cry. Then he was a sissy because he couldn't stop himself from crying; he was too scary.

The door opened and long hand reach in and pick up the empty plate. "Boy, I want the truth, did you tried to burn down Miss Louise's house?" "No, sir." Tom gave him a long look as if though he was trying to see if the boy was lying. "I want the truth?" "That's the true, sir." A worrisome look appears across the man's dark face. "Not only you, boy, but me and my family are in troubles along with you."

"Sir, this is the true, and you have got to believe me!" "How can I believe a word you said, when I don't even know you?" "Damn!"

Why me?" Why did you have to come to my house? "You can believe me, sir, I don't lie." Jim searched the man's face to see if he did. There was still doubt in his eyes. "Like I say, that's something I don't know, I don't know you."

"Miss Louise saw me knocking on her door, she got scary and dropped the lamp." "I know, and so do Will, he was there when it happening." He said it's still your fault because you didn't have no business at his mother house. What was you doing at that woman's house, boy, at that time of hour?" And I mean at the lady's front door, you're supposed to go to the back; you're either crazy or brave one!

"Ain't no one, even the ones in their wrong minds, not if they're colored, is going to be at a white person's house at that late hour."

He paused for a minute. "I'm like Will, you came there to do his mother harm." "No, I didn't, sir, and you've got to believe me." He gave the boy a long hard stare. Jim was the one that look away. "Why should I believe you, when you was at that woman's house at that time of hour?" You came there to robbed her? Or did you came to kill her?" "I'm not no murderer!" And I'm not no thief! If that was the case, why would I had knock? "You crazy, that's why you knocked."

"I knock because I thought I was at my grandmother's house." "Your mother's got a house like this, or she worked for someone who have got a house like Miss Louise's?"

"It's my grandmother's." "You know Will isn't going to take your word for it, he's got to see if for himself." He saw something in Jim expression and Jim stared down he didn't know what to do or say. "I'm trying to saved your tail,if I don't come up with some kind of excuse." He paused. "I ain't never lie to him before, if I don't every colored person that live

65

in this area is going to be here tomorrow and watch that man beats you, your back ain't gonna stand those licks." "I'll be back." He closed the door. Daylight shine through the cracks, giving Jim a little light. He's got to get out of here, please God, help me." His mouth begin to tremble and he put his hand over his eyes.

The door to the pen opened and it was Tom. Jim jumped and wipe his eyes quickly with his hands. He turned and faced the man, he could see it in his eyes that Tom knows he had been crying. He touched Jim's right shoulder. Jim took his hand and move Tom's hand from his shoulder. "I couldn't get Will to change his mind about you, Reebok, he said he couldn't let you get away, he was going to teach you a lesson." If he whipped you, he's going to kill you, I just know it, or hang you one." "Can you run?"

Jim nodded, wiping a wet streak from his cheek. "I'm scary. "I know, son, I am, too, because I don't know what me and my family are going to do." For my punishment, he's going to work me and my family in that field of his for six months without paid, I told him I couldn't make it like that. I have a family to take care of, and I told him I thought he was wrong for punishing me and my family for something you did."

He smiled. "It felt good standing up to that man." I mean it felt real good. So, he's going to work us for one month for fifty cent a day, that is half what he's paying me now." Jim frowned. "That ain't no money." "What are you talking about, boy, that's good money?" I owe it all to you, Reebok, standing up to Will the way I did, thanks." Now, I'm going to help you by getting you out of here. I want you to get out of that pen and run like you ain't never ran before. "Now get!"

Jim ran toward the large oak tree. He paused and look over his shoulders. "I love you, Mr. Tom!" "I love you, too, now get going, get!" There was no one sitting around the wishing tree. It was cloudy as if it was turning dim with the air a little chilly. Jim skipped around the large tree three times.

He was being carried by a large person. He squirms, trying to get out of the person's arms. "Now, since you've awaken boy, you can walk on to the house," said Jim's grandmother. "I went to your bedroom, but you wasn't in there." I search all through the house, calling you, and then something told me to go down to

Joe's store. And that's where I found you in your pajamas and robe with your arms around that big old tree, saying, "I can't let them cut down the wishing tree." "Now, you get your mind on that essay, and get it off that tree!" They're going to cut it down tomorrow."

"They can't, Grandma, I won't let them."

DRUGS — CHAPTER FOUR

Jim looked over his shoulders at the wishing tree with its branches full of leaves. It still was dark with the sky bringing in daylight. "It does works, he thought even if no one else didn't believe him. Now, thank to the wishing tree he knows what to write in his essay. He wished he could saved it.

He followed his grandma inside of the house. "Now, get on upstairs and work on that essay, so the school can announced it in the newspapers." You'd better not let Annie's grandson beats you, before that happening, I'll write it myself." "Grandma, this is my project, I'm going to write it."

He ran up the staircase halfway, and then he turned around. so that he was facing his grandmother as she stood in the hall. "Grandma, I'm not doing it because I was ask to, and believe it or not, I want to, now I do." Don't get disappointed if my essay doesn't appear in the newspapers, all I can do is my best."

When he said it his head was down. Jim swallowed the lump in his throat and raise his head. His grandma's face drooped with sadness. He met her eyes, eye that said he has took the joy out of it, and that far away look told him she knows that Annie's grandson would win. "Can you accepted that, Grandma?" "Yes, baby, as long as you do your best," she said as she entered her bedroom.

She shuts the door behind her and wiped a tear from her left eye. "Your best is not good enough,when it comes to Oscar, he's good at stuffs like that." He's going to win, I just knew it, and Annie's going to come over here, running, bragging about that,old grandson of hers, she makes me sick!" That is one day I won't open the door for her ass." She walked to the window, carrying her eyes to the two story house next door. "I wish she didn't live there. She spotted Jim running down the street. She raised the window and saw him to the oak tree. "C'mon here, boy, do I'm going to takes a belt to you!" Stop skipping around that tree!"

Jim ran down the street. The large oak tree stood tall and proud into the sky. Jim touched it and stare at it for a second as if though the tree could see him. He took his gaze off of it for a moment and stare down the road, because he heard his grandmother, calling his name at the top of her voice. He puts his gaze back on the tree. He smiled at it and began to skip around it three times. "Wishing tree, I wish you'd stay here forever, without anyone cutting you down, that's my wish." And for Joe to build another store somewhere else.

He jumped at the dark shadow. Jim moved around the large tree, letting its huge frame hide him from the intruder. The man sits down at the stump of the tree, lying his cane at his side. He was a heavyset man; even though he was sitting down Jim could tell he was tall, about six foot. He took a bottle from a paper bag and took a swallow. "Boy, I needed this." He then begin to talk as if he was talking to another person. "I could sleep right here all night, but I couldn't, the thought of how Old

Limp died at this same spot would keep me awake."

Jim came from his hiding place and sit beside the old man. "You couldn't sleep neither, huh?" Max asked. "You was saying something about Old Limp, that he died here?" "I was a little boy way back then, he was at this tree, and something must have shock him, from that day till this day, I still don't know what it was that made him died suddenly like that. That look was still on his face as he lay dead at this same tree." I wish I can go back to that day," the old man said.

"You can!" Jim exclaimed. "Just skip around this tree three times, and it will take you back there. "You've got to be kidding, an old ass man like me, skipping, I can just hardly walk with this cane."

"Mr. Max, the wishing tree worked, it really does!" "I use to believe that when I was a child, until one day we all were skipping, and I saw old Limp put some pennies by the tree. Old Limp would do that for us kids; so that we'd believes that the tree made our wishes came true. He took another swallow from the bottle. "Don't tell your grandma I'd been drinking, a man needs something sometimes to quiet him down, he needs companionship when he's real lonesome, and this stuff gives it to me."

He took the top off of the bottle and took a sip, I've got to save some for later. He put the top back on the bottle, now, remember, this is our little secrets." He handed the bottle to the boy. "C'mon, take a sip. "No, way, Grandma would skins me alive." "Who's gonna tell?" Not me, and I know you ain't. Take a sip; it will turns you into a man. "C'mon, Jim, a little bit won't hurt you, it'll make you sleep like a baby tonight."

"I ain't taking that stuff, my grandma would beat me to death." "Like I said, who's going to tell?" Just a little bit is not going to hurt you, it'll make you feels good." I'm talking about a little bit like this. He poured a drop into the tiny top. This little bit won't hardly wet your tongue, c'mon, take it."

Jim shook his head and stare down the road toward his house. "I can't." "She can't see you, not this far, and it's dark too." "I can't." "Why? How can this little bit hurts?" "Grandma told me and my brothers if we ever take alcohol, or smoke, or take drugs she was gonna beat us until we can't sits down for a month." She might be kind of old, but Grandma's beating hurts. And besides, she told us what that stuffs will do to a person."

He smiles, half of his front teethes were missing. "I know what it'll do to a person, it will makes a person feels good, I sure do at this moment."

Jim stares at him for a second. "That's because you're drunk!" "My grandma told me and my brothers that alcohol reaches the brain almost as soon as it is drunk. It depresses the brain, slowing down the work of the nervous system. She said the brain loses its ability to control the mind and body. "I don't want that stuff in me."

"Your grandma didn't even finished the third grade, can't even read, how do she know so much about alcohol?" "Don't know shit!" Hell, she used to swim in it, damn ass couldn't hardly stand up, she'd be so damn drunk. To one of the houses across the street all the lights went out. "Let me ask you something. "If you'd just take a little bit, how would she know?"

"I would know, and when I couldn't look my grandma in the eye, she'll know, because I'll feel so guilty for breaking her trust." And that would hurt me more than anything to see

her hurts like that. Grandma took me and my

two brothers in when no one else wouldn't take

us. She said she didn't want to see us be put in

a home, and she was going to raised us the best

way she can. She say I'm going to raised you

boys the same way my daddy raised me, if

y'all gets out of hand, I'm going to tear your

asses up with that damned belt, because if I

don't do it I know who's going to. "Once y'all

gets behind that jail cell, you'll be raised then.

I love you boys too much to see that happens

to y'all. And she told us, she can't give us

much, but she can gives us love and do the best she can by us."

He took a pack of cigarettes from his shirt pocket; took a match and lit ones. The man draws on it and let the smoke out through his nostrils. He handed it to the boy. Jim shook his head. "No way, "my Grandma told us never to smoke. She told us, just one cigarette causes cigarette breath" and dulls the taste buds. She said the hot smoke is harmful to the mouth and throat tissues. And that cigarette smoking plays a major role in causing cancer of the oral cavity and larynx." She said tar stains the teeth, causing brown spots."

I don't want to hear no more what your grandma had to said, she can't scare me, I'd been smoking for years, it ain't nothing wrong with me, if anything, it relax me real good. "What are you looking at?" the man asked. He took another draw from the half smoke cigarette and throw it down, it fell to the shoulder of the road. "Cigarette breath, I can't believe she called me that. No wonder she didn't want to kiss me." What else did she had to say about smoking?"

"She told us with each puff of a cigarette, a smoker comes in contact with more than 3,000 chemicals. Tobacco contains nicotine, a poisonous drug stimulant that acts on the adrenal glands and heart tissue." She said it is responsible for the rise in blood pressure and the increase in heartbeat that results from smoking a cigarette."

He took out another cigarette. "Mr. Max, what happened to Old Limp?" He took a puff first before answering. He just died of a heart attack when he saw something at this tree. "I was watching him that day, I was behind the store." He was blowing that old harmonica of his, and then he started singing. The old man began to sang the song. "Skip around the wishing tree, skip three times, make your wish." And then Old Limp stood up with his cane, I remember it just like it had happening yesterday. He walked toward the store and then he stopped; reach in his pockets, and then he pulled his pockets out so that it were hanging outside of his pants. "And then he came back to the tree, he walked around it three times." I was a little boy, but I remember it so good. "Help me get up boy so I can go home."

Jim has a strange look on his face as if though he was in a trance. "I know what happening!" He was talking more to himself than he was to the man. "He was going to the store to buy himself something, he put his hands in his pockets and realize he didn't have no money." When Old Limp walked around the wishing tree three times, what did he wished for?" Jim asked. "Help me up first." He was trying to wobbly to his feet with his cane.

"I dunno, "Max said. "But there was a lot of coins at the stump of this tree, and the way Old Limp was looking at it; like he couldn't believed it were there. "It fells from his pockets." The boy and the man begin to walks down the road. Jim held the man by the arm with his other hand the man has the cane, walking as slowly as he could. "No, it didn't, sir, those coins were at that tree because Old

Limp wished for it. "That's what kill him, shock."

He left his bedroom and ran down the narrow staircase. He was getting ready to knock on his grandmother's bedroom door when she opened it, dressed in her robe. She yawned. "Grandma, Joe changed his mind about cutting down the wishing tree, didn't he?" Please let she said yes, thinking about that wish he had made. "Yes, Joe did change his mind, it was in the papers a week ago; he's going to build a new store on Main Street." He said cutting down that large oak tree wouldn't attract customers no more, they loves to sits under its huge shade." "In fact, in four days Joe is having a park party at the wishing tree."

She paused, still standing at her room door. "Did you finish your essay?" "You know on Sundays when we comes from church, me, Annie, Sally, Sue, and Beth sits under that wishing tree, drinking sodas, and just talking, having fun." They all lives on the same street we do. Well, this last past Sunday, the girls started to brags about how good their grandsons essays were, and they knows it were going to be in the newspapers. So we made a bet, whomever grandson's essay be in the paper the grandmother will get a hundred dollars. And then they all turns to me, and says did Jim finished his essay? I said yes. And they asks what year. I say, 1948. "You made me lie on Sunday, boy!" "Now, did you finished your essay?"

Jim swallowed and stare down. "No, ma'am." "I'm going to beat you." Jim raised his head. The look in his grandmother's eyes scare him, he hadn't never seen her that anger. "I've got until tomorrow to bring it in." "Don't beat me."

"Get in that room!" She stepped aside so Jim could go in her room. "Take off your robe, and pull down your pajamas!" "It will hurt,

Grandma." "That's what I want it to do!" Lean over that chair."

Jim closed his eyes and held on tight to the arm of the chairarm. The first lick made him rise up and grit his teeth. The second one made him scream out. "Please don't hit me no more, Grandma!" But she didn't listen but kept on hitting him. "You get on up that stair and get ready for school, and when you come home, you'd better do that essay'."

. He pulled up his pajamas, grab his robe from the chair. Jim puts it on. "Grandma, I did my essay, I just haven't finish it." He wiped at his eyes and walk toward the door. "When I ask you, you say no." "You asked me did I finish it, that's what I was saying no to." once again he wiped at his eyes, but the tears kept coming. When he opened the door his two brothers stood in the hall, listening at the door. They met their grandma's eyes and ran upstairs. "Get up there and get ready for school, all three of y'all!" When Jim got to the top of the stair he heard his grandmother said, "I'm sorry, Jim." He answered her with a sob.

JIM'S ESSAY — CHAPTER FIVE

My class and I was asked by our fourth grade teacher, Mrs. Webb to write a ten pages essay about what took place in the year of 1900, 1910, and on up to 1960s, and how it was different from the 1990s. I decide to write my essay about the year of 1950, about segregation. How it begin and how it was struggle for civil rights. I'm not writing it to brings up a lot of bad unpleasant memories, but appreciate.

At one point in my life segregation didn't mean nothing to me. Why should it? It didn't happening to me. I didn't know what segregation meant, and I didn't know how it felt like to be treated inferior. But now I realize it's a very important part of history, which I will always be grateful to. That's why I decide to name the title of my essay, Gratitude. If it weren't for people like Martin Luther King, Jr., Rosa Parks, Malcolm X, and other black leaders struggled to end segregation black would still be in bounden and inferior, and so would I. I thank God for choosing a great man like Martin Luther King, Jr., through him blacks have a chance of being equal. He didn't let racial slurred stopped him from fighting for civil rights for you and me. He didn't let threat on his life stop him from fighting for civil rights. He didn't let spending time in jail stop him from fighting for civil rights for you and me. And yet, through all those brutal attempts to stop him, he never once use violent. His nonviolence demonstration against racial inequality, was awarded to him the Nobel Peace prize in 1964.

Yes, I am honor and proud to have known of a great man like Martin Luther King, Jr. Gratitude, yes, I am, because his courage and success have giving me and you a chance to become somebody one day. And to not to let what he did go in vain. I don't want no part of hatred. Yes, there is still hatred and prejudice still haunting American Streets, but not as bad as it was before. on those haunted street, so many bloodshed, so many lives have been lost; so much pain and heartache. I hope one day it will be erase with gratitude.

Segregation have started a long time ago when the thirteen amendment had outlawed slavery in 1865, but many white Southerners had never been able to regard blacks as their equals or even as citizen of the United States. Slavery was replaced from the rest of society. Under segregation, black children could not go to the same schools as white children, and blacks were not allowed to use the same public facilities. Such as, hotels, theaters, restaurants, lunch counters, sinks, bathrooms, water fountains, waiting rooms, libraries, park, swimming pools, as white people. Black were also not allowed the same access to public transportation as whites. black passengers couldn't sit with a white person or across the aisle from them. A black passenger would have to go to the back of the bus if a white passenger need a seat. A black passenger would have to give up he or she seat to that passenger.

Marjorie Darcene Person

When Rosa Parks did not gave up her bus seat to a white passenger in December of 1955, she was taken the first step so all blacks could be equal to whites. Yes, I'm graceful because she took the pain for me and you. I myself didn't have to faced that kind of treatment, pain that makes you feels like you isn't nobody, that makes you feels like you are poison. The kind of pain that will brings tears to one eyes when one's feeling is hurts, but it goes way beyond that. Back in those days blacks were treating like they didn't have no feelings at all.

It takes one person to make a difference, and she made that difference a long time ago by refusing to give up her bus seat. It led to Martin Luther King's boycott campaign of the bus company and to the campaign for civil rights. If I could shake Rosa Parks' hand, I'd do it with proudness and gladness on my face. Long then, even though if black did have a good education and were qualify to do the job they couldn't get hire. The only job that blacks could get was the one that whites turn down, such as housecleaning, garbage man, babysitting, cooking, sewer maintenance, sewing, and working in the fields.

Gratitude, yes, I am. I thank God for people like Martin Luther King for giving you and me a chance to become somebody someday, and to be equal to white. When I grow up I want to be a doctor, and thank to Martin Luther King I got that chance because segregation no longer hang over my head. And I will do my best to keep segregation out of my life. What I meant by that, by not letting hatred enter my body and corrupt my mind. No, I will not allow it, and doesn't want no part of it. And I hope one day it will be erase along with prejudice, drugs. It was brought here for that reason to keep you still in bounden, to keep you still in segregation, but only drugs are worsen than that. It doesn't make you be treated like you're nobody; it turns you into one, until everything around you is destroyed including you, yourself, because it'll destroy a person's life, a person's dreams, a person's plans to make something out of themselves.

The large crowd, by the hundreds marched in the freedom march, including schoolchildren, marching for freedom. The anger spectators did everything they could do to stop the marchers. Some of them were even throw in jail, but that didn't stop the rest of the marchers they kept on going, refusing to let anything stop them. vicious insults, threat, brutally beaten didn't stop the rest of the marchers they were determined to keep going, marching for freedom. In one of those speeches Martin Luther King say. "I have a dream that one day little white girls will be holding little negro girls' hands, little white boys will be holding little negro boys' hands. His beautiful dream came true.

Gratitude, yes I am. If I could shake Martin Luther King's hand I would do it with proudness and honor on my face. And I'd said. "Thank you so very much, thank you, sir, for not letting me face segregation. What you did I will not let it go in vain, because I'm determined to make something out of myself. I thank God for choosing a great man like you to lead us to freedom. In the 60s there was a great deal of hate between black and white. When Martin Luther King won the fight for segregation, most of that hate gradually erased. And what is left I hope one day that, too, will be erased with gratitude. The difference from the 90s and the 50s, segregation no longer exist, and a person can marry any race he or she chooses.

Now, I have a dream, and I hope one day it will come true. That on every corner it will be a vacancy that will teach kids how to say no to drugs, instead of teaching them how to say yes to it. It will be a place where kids can hang out at just to get them out of the street. It will be a place where they can play games, how to trained themselves to say no to drugs. It will be a building where mentors teaches them how to make something out of themselves, and to hang in there no matter what kind of obstacles they're facing.

Whether you're black, white, brown, yellow, red. If anyone would offer you drugs or alcohol just say thanks, but no thank. I have a dream, and that dream is to make something out of myself. If I'll take that stuff I can say goodbye to my dreams because it will be destroy along with everything else in my life. No matter what my situations are like, with God's help and great determination, my dreams will become a reality one day.

Jim stood at his bedroom window, staring down the street at the large oak tree. He thanks God Joe changed his mind. Jim knew it were Joe's customers that convinced him to change his mind. He smiles as if though he was remembering, it weren't them it was the wish he'd granted. He jumped when he heard his grandma's voice, calling his name loudly upstairs. "I'm coming, Grandma!" What did I do? He could hear it in her voice. Probably one of his brothers have did something and put it on him so he could takes the blame. "Those rats, I'll bet that's what happening. Did they ate the last piece of grandma's chocolate cake, and told her I ate it?" "Or did they, but his thoughts were interrupt by his grandma. "Come here, right now, Jim!" He put his hands behind him and touch his butt, his eyes stung with tears, thinking about that large belt she was going to beat him with. "I'm coming!" His grandma was downstairs, standing in the hall with a foot on the first step of the staircase, her hand was behind her back. Jim knows whenever she was in that position she has a large switch or belt behind her, and sometimes gifts. But he and his brothers get more whipping than they do gifts.

"Stop crying, and come on down here!" "I didn't do it, Grandma, I swear I didn't." "Stop crying." He stepped down slowly, wiping his eyes. Why was she dressed like that? He ain't never seen his grandma dress up like that, except on Sundays. Her eyes have a smile in them with a funny look on her face as if she was staring at him with love in her eyes. Seeing her like that his fear ease a little.

"I call you down here to show you this."

She removed her arm from behind her back, in her hand she was holding a newspaper. Jim's eyes grew big. "I won!" "My essay won, for real?" He took the paper from her hand and begin to read it. Beside Jim's picture it was a full page story about his essay. "I can't believe it, Grandma, I won, I won, I really did!"

"Can Grandma have a hug, I mean a big one?" Jim went into her arms. "Grandma loves you very much, she do, baby, so much." "Grandma, can I go back reading the paper?" She took her arms from her grandson and wipe her eyes with a handkerchief. "I bought all the newspapers that Joe have in his store. "Don and Paul are out now, giving them to friends and relations." I made sure they took one over to Annie's, you know I have to do that," she laughed. Gosh, that made my day! Later on I'm going over there, and I'm going to take a newspaper with me, in case she didn't get one."

Jim didn't glance up from the paper but kept on reading it. "Wow!" he says as he smiled. "My picture is beside it, Grandma." "Wow!" "That's not all," she said, smiling. "Someone from the evening news will be over here in less than an hour to interview you." Jim dropped the newspaper, he stood there with his face frown up. "For what?" "Your essay," Alice May said. "Mrs. Webb said whoever essay win will be in the newspaper, not on television, you mean she lied?"

"No, Jim, she didn't lie, it suppose to be in the newspaper only, but you didn't only written an essay, you written a message, too, that's why they want to put it on television." "I wish I have known, I wouldn't never had written it like that!" "Don't be scary, baby." "I am, Grandma." "And that's not all." She sent it to her brother, who's a publisher. She smiles and jump slightly. "This is what he sent you."

Jim took the check. "That much?" She nodded.

"Grandma is so proud of you, baby, so proud."
She wiped at her eyes.

He handed the check back to her. She stares
at it for a moment. "Who would have thought
I'll be getting something this big in the mail."
There is a God, I pray for this a many nights,
for God to bless me with enough money to pay
these bills, and to get out of this house. Lord I
thank you, I thank you Lord." Now I can buy
that house on Cherry Lane, get that bike for
you, those drum for Don, and a car for Paul.
"You've made your grandma so happy, I wish
your mother was here to see what a fine young

man you turn out to be. "Give grandma another hug, I mean a big one."

He put his arms around his grandma. "Grandma, I can't breath!" "Baby, let grandma gets one more hug from you." I can hug you until I can't hug you no more, I'm so proud of you," she says as she kissed his cheek. "I mean it, Jim, I'm so proud. "Let me hug you one more time."

Down by the wishing tree to the park there were a large crowd, helping Joe celebrate his second store. There were three men with instruments, two of them have violins, and then there was one man with a harmonica. Joe has the mike in his hand talking proudly. "We're not here only to celebrate my new store, but also to celebrate a celebrity in our town, Jim Perry!" The large crowd applaud. "How many of y'all saw Jim on television last night?" Every hand out there raise.

"I recorded it and played it five more times. The crowd laughs. "Every time I past that corner, I'll see fifteen or twenty guys, but now, I only see six." And most of them that used to hang on that corner were young boys, sixteen and on up, and some even younger. Thank to Jim's marvelous essay, some of them have stops. And one of them even ask me for a job the other day. I hire him. He met Jim's gaze into the crowd. Jim's essay might not help everyone, but thank God for the ones it is helping. The large crowd applaud once again. "You wrote your essay like that for me, didn't you?" Oscar asked. Jim stares at him with opening mouth. He wanted to said no, but couldn't. "Thank for caring that much."

The music went in the air and the man with the harmonica did the singing. "Skip around the wishing tree, skip three times round the wishing tree. Jim was doing the skip dance with his grandma, but they were walking it while three other couples were doing the skip dance., They did everything the man told them to do until they were four foot away with the boys' backs facing the girls'. They begin to skip backward until their backs were touching each other. "Now stand beside your partners. The four couples continues skipping, standing beside their mates. Now change partner by pointing to someone in the crowd.

Jim pointed to a white girl and she skipped to him, and took him by the arm. Alice May pointed at Old Max. He shook his head. "Get somebody else!" "I'm too old to be skipping."

"C'mon here, we can walk it." "And look like fools!" All I came here for to eat some of that good food, and sit under all that shade."

He sits down and lay his cane beside him. Alice May stood beside him, rocking her large body slightly. She stares into the crowd, watching the girls skipped around their partners.

Old Max pulled on the hem of Alice May's dress. "Go fix me a plate, old lady, and don't forget to put some chicken wings on it." "I didn't came here to work, I came here to dance, even if I have to walk it, that's what I'm doing to do, and I'm not going to do it alone.." "What about my plate?" He holler after her.

"Fix it yourself, and fix me one too, old man."

"Who are you calling, old, old woman!"

Jim stares toward the wishing tree Old Max wasn't there, he saw a young man resembled Old max a great deal as if though he was Old Max identical twin. He watch the man as he left the tree and ask Alice May for a dance.

About The Author

Marjorie Darcene Person was born in Washington county to Miss Helen Person. She is divorced with two daughters. She loves to write, especially inspiring stories. She doesn't write to lecture, but rather to give someone out there hope and encouragement. That's why she loves doing it.

www.ingramcontent.com/pod-product-compliance
Lightning Source LLC
Chambersburg PA
CBHW051440280526
45785CB00003B/1371